# The Blackfeet

## by Petra Press

Content Adviser: Professor Sherry L. Field,
Department of Social Science Education, College of Education,
The University of Georgia

Reading Adviser: Dr. Linda D. Labbo,
Department of Reading Education, College of Education,
The University of Georgia

 **COMPASS POINT BOOKS**

Minneapolis, Minnesota

Compass Point Books
3722 West 50th Street, #115
Minneapolis, MN 55410

Visit Compass Point Books on the Internet at *www.compasspointbooks.com* or e-mail your request
to *custserv@compasspointbooks.com*

Photographs ©: Marilyn "Angel" Wynn, cover, 4, 5, 15, 16, 17, 23, 31, 39; XNR Productions, Inc.,
6; William B. Folsom, 7; Stock Montage/The Newberry Library, 9, 10, 14, 21, 28; Science
VU/Visuals Unlimited, 11; Archive Photos, 12, 30, 38; Brian Parker/Tom Stack and Associates,
13; Dan Polin, 18; North Wind Picture Archives, 19 (top and bottom), 32; Hulton Getty/Archive
Photos, 20, 22, 24, 25, 26, 29; Oregon Trail Museum Association, 27; Denver Public Library,
Western History Collection, 36–37; George Wuerthner, 40, 41 (top and bottom); Unicorn Stock
Photos/Bob Coury, 42; Jan Lucie, 43.

Editors: E. Russell Primm, Emily J. Dolbear, and Alice K. Flanagan
Photo Researcher: Svetlana Zhurkina
Photo Selector: Alice K. Flanagan
Designer: Bradfordesign, Inc.

**Library of Congress Cataloging-in-Publication Data**
Press, Petra.
    The Blackfeet / by Petra Press.
       p. cm. — (First reports)
    Includes bibliographical references and index.
    ISBN 0-7565-0078-8 (hardcover : lib. bdg.)
    1. Siksika Indians—History—Juvenile literature. 2. Siksika Indians—Social life and customs—
Juvenile literature. [1. Siksika Indians. 2. Indians of North America.] I. Title. II. Series.
    E99.S54 B54 2001
    978'.004973—dc21                                                    00-011065

# Table of Contents

# The Blackfeet Nation

▲ *The Blackfeet Nation is in Montana.*

Three American Indian tribes make up the Blackfeet
Nation—the Piegan, the Blood, and the Blackfeet. A
nation is an American Indian tribe or group of tribes
under one government.

CANADA

Alberta

British
Columbia

Saskatchewan

Ontario

Lake
Winnipegosis

Lake Winnipeg

Lake
Manitoba

Lake
of the
Woods

Manitoba

Wa.

Missouri

North
Dakota

Montana

Minnesota

Wis.

Idaho

South Dakota

UNITED STATES

Mississippi

Wyoming

Missouri

Great
Salt Lake

Nebraska

Iowa

Nevada

Utah

Colorado

Blackfeet lands at time
of European contact

Present-day
Blackfeet Reservation

0    100    200 miles

0    100    200 kilometers

▲ The present-day Blackfeet Reservation and the traditional homelands

The Piegan (pronounced pay-GAN) people live on the Blackfeet **Reservation** in Montana. A reservation is an area of land that a government sets aside for people to live on. Sometimes, the Piegan are called the Pikuni.

The second tribe in the Blackfeet Nation is the Blood. The Blood are also known as the Kainah (KAY-nah). They live on reserves in Alberta, Canada. In Canada, reservations are called reserves.

The Blackfeet, or Siksika (SIHK-sih-kah), are the third tribe. They also live on reserves in Alberta, Canada.

Some of the customs of the three Blackfeet groups are different. But they all speak the same

▲ *Blackfeet Ronnie Ligget lives on Browning Reservation in Montana.*

language. And they share many similar beliefs and traditions.

Some people believe that the Blackfeet got their name from the **moccasins** they wore. They painted the bottoms black. Or the moccasins may have turned black in prairie fires.

# Traveling Hunters

▲ A Blackfeet camp

Long ago, the Blackfeet lived far to the east in a wooded area north of the Great Lakes. They did not get along with their neighbors, the Cree Indians. So, in the 1600s, the Blackfeet decided to move west to the **Great Plains**.

▲ *A Blackfeet sled called a travois from the late nineteenth century*

The Indians did not have horses at that time. It was a long trip on foot. Along the way, dogs carried their things. The dogs pulled a sled called a **travois**.

On the Great Plains, the Blackfeet became **nomadic hunters**. Nomadic hunters move from place to place. They travel in groups called **bands**.

The Blackfeet moved around the plains looking for buffalo, or bison. They hunted the buffalo on foot. A band of hunters would circle a herd of buffalo near a cliff. They would scare the animals into running over the cliff.

Later, the Blackfeet learned to ride horses. Then they hunted buffalo on horseback.

▲ Blackfeet hunted buffalo by driving them over cliffs.

Hundreds of years ago, great herds of buffalo roamed the Great Plains. At one time, as many as 60 million buffalo may have lived on the prairies.

▲ *Riding horses made buffalo-hunting easier for the Blackfeet.*

Buffalo were very important to the Blackfeet. They used every part of the buffalo in their daily lives. No part of a buffalo was left unused.

▲ *Buffalo in South Dakota*

# Women's Work

While the men hunted, the women gathered roots, berries, and other wild plants. They took care of the camp and the children. They made all of the meals and all of the clothing.

▲ *While the men hunted, women gathered berries and roots.*

▲ *Decorating a belt with seed beads*

When the men returned with meat, the women prepared it. They roasted the meat over campfires or dried it for later use. They **tanned** the buffalo skins. Then they sewed them together to make moccasins, robes, and other warm clothing. They lived in tents, or tepees, made from the skins.

Women used the stringy muscles along the backbone of the buffalo as thread. They braided buffalo hair into ropes and belts. From the bones, they carved toys, tools, and sewing needles. From the

▲ *Materials needed by the Blackfeet to make arrows*

▲ *A cooking pot made from buffalo hide*

horns, they made spoons and cups. The stomach and bladder were used as containers for carrying food and water.

And buffalo fat made good soap. Even buffalo droppings were used. Dried buffalo droppings kept campfires burning.

# The Sun Dance

Today, the buffalo is still a very important animal to the Blackfeet. Many of the Blackfeet ceremonies honor the spirit of the buffalo. Every year, the Blackfeet have a special celebration called the Sun Dance. At the Sun Dance, the buffalo holds a special place of honor.

▲ *The buffalo is still important to Blackfeet celebrations.*

In the past, all the hunting bands got together during the summer. They looked forward to the week-

▲ *A traditional way to tame horses*

▲ *Worship ceremonies were important to the Blackfeet.*

long Sun Dance. It was a time to trade and to share news. It was a time to dance, sing, and celebrate. But it was also a time for prayer and ceremony.

▲ *The ritual of the Sun Dance*

Like many Plains Indians, the Blackfeet believed in a Great Spirit. They prayed often to him. During the Sun Dance, many people took part in activities that were painful. They cut parts of their bodies and danced in the hot sun. They wanted to prove their bravery. They believed the Sun Dance would help to get their prayers heard.

▲ *A dance honoring the buffalo*

Some people asked the Great Spirit to help them be great warriors or hunters. Others asked him to protect their families against sickness or danger. The Sun Dance is still an important part of life for all of the Blackfeet.

# Trappers and Warriors

▲ *The Blackfeet were a powerful people.*

In the 1700s, the Blackfeet grew stronger. They became one of the most powerful American Indian tribes in North America.

▲ *Animal hides for trading*

The Blackfeet Indians watched as white trappers and traders came onto their land. They saw them trap beaver. They saw them get rich by selling the beaver furs. Before long, the traders were building trading posts.

The Blackfeet did not like the traders. But they liked the things they traded.

▲ *Bringing hides to the trading post*

Soon the Blackfeet hunters began to bring their buffalo skins and beaver furs to the trading posts. In return, the Indians got beads, blankets, horses, guns, and other things.

With horses and guns, the Blackfeet soon became

the best riders on the Great Plains. They drove away enemy tribes.

By the 1800s, the Blackfeet were a nation of warriors. Everyone was afraid of them.

▲ *Blackfeet warriors were much feared.*

# Disease and Hunger

In the 1830s, the Blackfeet Nation became smaller. American fur traders began opening trading posts on the Missouri River. Then settlers arrived.

Along with the white settlers came a disease called smallpox. It killed nearly 6,000 Blackfeet.

▲ *White settlers brought diseases that killed many Indians.*

▲ *Large herds of buffalo once roamed the Great Plains.*

That was more than two-thirds of the entire Blackfeet people.

Then white hunters began shooting buffalo. They skinned the animals and left the meat to rot. Some people paid hunters $3.50 for every buffalo they shot and skinned. Later, some hunters shot the buffalo for sport. They did not even take the hides. No one did anything to stop them.

By the late 1800s, the buffalo had almost disappeared. And the Blackfeet were beginning to die from hunger.

▲ *Large buffalo herds such as these were disappearing.*

# Broken Promises

▲ *A Blackfeet camp*

White settlers kept coming west. Many whites settled along the Missouri River, where the Blackfeet lived. Always, Indians and settlers fought over the land. The U.S. government made several **treaties**, or agreements, with the Blackfeet to stop the fighting.

▲ *The U.S. government promised to feed the Blackfeet.*

But with each treaty, the U.S. government took more and more Blackfeet land. In return, the U.S. government promised to feed, educate, and care for the Blackfeet Nation. It set aside an area for the Blackfeet to live on. Then it opened the rest of the land to white settlers.

The U.S. government broke most of its promises to the Blackfeet Nation. By the mid-1880s, no buffalo were left to hunt. Now the Blackfeet had to depend on the U.S. government for all of their food, shelter, and supplies.

During the hard winter of 1883, the Blackfeet never got their government supplies. Without food and heat, 600 Blackfeet died.

▲ *Many Blackfeet suffered during the winter of 1883.*

# Farming the Land

▲ *The Dawes Allotment Act gave small family farms to Indians.*

In the late 1800s, some government and religious groups set up schools on the reservation. Then Congress passed a law. It made the Indians live on small family farms. Each family received about 160 acres (65 hectares) of reservation land.

The U.S. government kept the rest of the land or sold it to white settlers. Some of this land is now Glacier National Park in Montana.

The government believed that farming would help the Blackfeet live on their own. But the Blackfeet had always been hunters. They knew little about farming or raising cattle. So not many Blackfeet learned to farm well.

▲ *The U.S. government believed that farming was the answer to the Blackfeet's problems.*

▲ *The Blackfeet learned to improve the harvest.*

Then in 1919, dry weather ruined the crops. The Blackfeet Indians who were farming lost much of their harvest. Most of the Blackfeet had to sell their land just to pay their taxes.

WHY PAY RENT?

Better Own a FARM ❦ Start NOW!

1895

**Thousands of Acres** of fertile lands, capable of raising the finest quality of farm products in luxurious abundance.

Are FOR SALE, Upon Reasonable Terms

In Wisconsin, Minnesota, South Dakota, Iowa, Nebraska, and Wyoming. Reference to reliable statistics will demonstrate the fact that the pursuits of agriculture, stock-raising, and dairying in these States are attended with profitable results.

THE NORTH-WESTERN LINE

**CHICAGO & NORTH-WESTERN RAILWAY**

Affords EASY Access to Unfailing Markets

Correspondence solicited from intending settlers.

Send for free copy of *The North-Western Home Seeker.*

H. R. McCULLOUGH,
General Traffic Manager.

W. B. KNISKERN,
Gen'l Pass'r and Ticket Agt.

CHICAGO.

▲ As the Blackfeet gave up their farms, Easterners moved west.

35

# A Lost Way of Life

Land was not the only thing the Blackfeet had to give up. The U.S. government began taking away all the things that made the Blackfeet proud to be Blackfeet.

The Blackfeet were not allowed to practice their religion. They were not allowed to follow their traditions. The children were taken away from their families and sent to **boarding schools**. They were not allowed to speak their language or wear traditional

▲ *Blackfeet women line up for government supplies.*

clothes. The children were taught a new religion and a new way of life.

On the reservation, living conditions were terrible. Few people had jobs. Most people were dying from hunger.

▲ *The Blackfeet were urged to give up their traditions.*

▲ *Traditional Blackfeet arts*

Life began to improve in 1934. That was the year the U.S. Congress passed the Indian Reorganization Act. Then the Blackfeet set up a tribal government. They opened businesses, such as a pencil factory. And they began to believe again in the beauty of their art and their traditions.

# The Blackfeet Today

▲ *The Blackfeet Reservation in Montana*

Today, the Blackfeet Nation has more than 30,000 members. Some live and work in cities. But most Blackfeet still live on reservations in the United States and Canada.

Blackfeet Indians are farmers and ranchers. They are teachers and nurses. Some people work in the

▲ Some Blackfeet have
ranches and farms.

▼ Oil production on the
Blackfeet Reservation

▲ *Many tourists travel through the Blackfeet Reservation to get to Glacier National Park.*

forests on the reservation. Others work at the pencil factory. Many Blackfeet work at the oil and gas reserves on the reservation. The tribal government sells most of its oil and gas to large energy companies.

Every year, tourists drive through the Blackfeet Reservation to get to Glacier National Park in Montana. They stop at Blackfeet campgrounds. And they

▲ *Dancing at their annual celebration in July*

visit museums and gift shops. Some tourists come to see the **rodeos**. Many take part in the North American Indian Days Celebration held every July.

Like other Americans, the Blackfeet want a good life for their children. They want them to be happy and successful. They know it will take hard work. And they are working together to make it happen.

# Glossary

**bands**—groups of people who live and travel together

**boarding schools**—places where meals and rooms are provided to students

**Great Plains**—the big prairies in the western United States and Canada

**moccasins**—soft leather shoes

**nomadic hunters**—people who travel from place to place to hunt and gather food

**reservation**—a large area of land set aside for Native Americans; in Canada, reservations are called reserves

**rodeos**—shows or contests in which people ride horses, rope calves, and perform other skills used by cowboys

**tan**—to make an animal skin soft

**travois**—a sled pulled by dogs or horses

**treaties**—agreements between two governments

# Did You Know?

- When the Blackfeet saw horses for the first time they called them "elk dogs."

- The first business the Blackfeet Tribal Business Council created in 1935 was a pencil factory.

- An American artist named Charles Russell became famous for his paintings of Blackfeet life in the late 1800s.

- Every July, Native Americans take part in a four-day Indian Days Celebration at the Blackfeet Tribal Fairgrounds.

- In Canada, the Blackfeet are usually called the Blackfoot.

# At a Glance

**Tribal name:** Blackfeet

**Divisions:** Blackfeet, Blood, Piegan

**Past locations:** Montana; Saskatchewan and Alberta in Canada

**Present locations:** Montana; Alberta, Canada

**Traditional houses:** Tepees

**Traditional clothing material:** Skins

**Traditional transportation:** Horses

**Traditional food:** Meat, wild plants

# Important Dates

| | |
|---|---|
| **1730–1750** | Blackfeet start hunting on horseback. |
| **1781** | A smallpox outbreak kills hundreds of Blackfeet. |
| **1837** | A second smallpox outbreak kills nearly 6,000 Blackfeet. |
| **1855** | A treaty between the Blackfeet and the U.S. government marks out the Blackfeet Nation. |
| **1870** | U.S. soldiers kill 200 Blackfeet and capture 140 women and children at the Marias River in Montana. |
| **1872** | The first school for Blackfeet children opens at Teton River Agency in Montana. |
| **1883–1884** | About 600 Blackfeet die from hunger during the winter and spring. |
| **1919** | Dry weather ruins Blackfeet crops. |
| **1934** | The Blackfeet set up a tribal government. |
| **1982** | The U.S. government pays the Blackfeet Nation $29 million. |
| **1994** | The Blackfeet adopt Pikuni as its official language. |

# Want to Know More?

### At the Library

Hahn, Elizabeth. *The Blackfoot*. Vero Beach, Fla.: Rourke Press, 1992.

Hendrickson, Ann-Marie. *The Blackfeet Indians*. New York: Junior Library of Chelsea House, 1997.

Lacey, Theresa Jensen. *The Blackfeet*. New York: Chelsea House, 1995.

Linderman, Frank Bird. *Blackfeet Indians*. New York: Gramercy Books, 1995.

### On the Web

**Official Site of the Blackfeet Nation**
*http://www.blackfeetnation.com*
For information about the culture and history of the tribe

**Indian Nations of Montana: Blackfeet**
*http://lewisandclark.state.mt.us/blackfeet.htm*
For current information about the tribe

### Through the Mail

**Blackfeet Nation**
P.O. Box 850
Browning, MT 59417
To get information about the Blackfeet Reservation

### On the Road

**Museum of the Plains Indian**
Just off U.S. 89 in Browning, MT
406/338-2230
To see exhibits of Northern Plains Indians and an authentic re-creation of a Blackfeet encampment

# Index

**About the Author**

Petra Press is a freelance writer of young adult non-fiction, specializing in the diverse culture of the Americas. Her more than twenty books include histories of U.S. immigration, education, and settlement of the West, as well as portraits of numerous indigenous cultures. She lives with her husband, David, in Milwaukee, Wisconsin.